DRESSOLOGY

words for how we wear

Sophie Lewis

GREAT
CURVE

There just aren't enough words in the English dictionary to truly describe the complex relationship we all have with our clothes.

This small book will go some way to help you and your sartorial sisters articulate those daily clothing dramas, quibbles and delights.

It's the best accessory your vocabulary could wish for.

Dressology

ANTI-SHOECIAL

[an-ti-shu-shal]

Shoes that are unable to mix with any
of your existing wardrobe but still demand
you buy them.

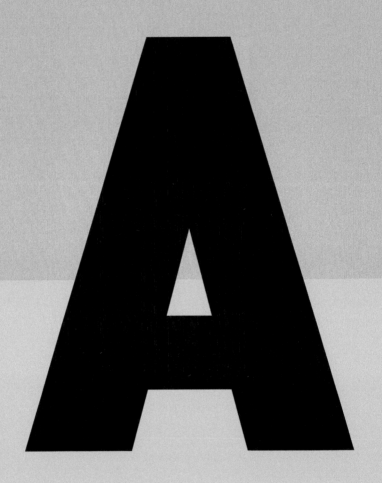

Dressology

AFTER-SHORTS

[arf-ter-sh-orts]

Those doubts that come the minute you
leave the house bare-legged for the first
time this summer.

Dressology

AUTUMNISTIC

[or-tum-nis-tic]

When the new season's cosy knits and coats actually make you look forward to the end of summer.

B

BETWINI

[be-twee-nee]

Finding great new swimwear but the size up
is too big and the size down is too small.
Grrrr.

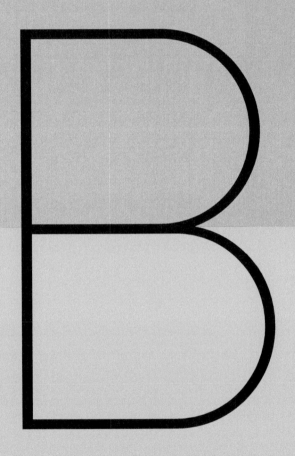

Dressology

BLUEO

[bloo-oh]

Realising that one drop of sweat changes
your perfect blue top from cornflower to
cobalt. Oh god.

Dressology

BARGAINBLURT

[bar-gan-blurt]

The unexplainable urge to tell anyone who
admires your outfit how little it cost.

Dressology

BRA-MNESTY

[brah-am-nest-tee]

Finally freeing your boobs at the end of the day from a particularly uncomfortable bra.

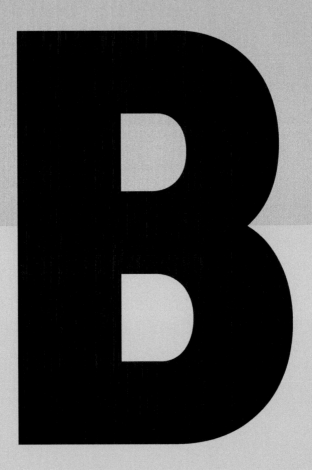

Dressology

BOOMERANGBLACK

[boo-mer-rang-bl-ack]

When you flirt with wearing a bright stand-
out outfit to an event but get cold feet
at the last minute and go back to that staple
black dress instead.

Dressology

CRYRONING

[cri-oh-ning]

The large pile of clothes that you
have avoided wearing because
they need ironing.
And you hate ironing.

C

CROTCHWHISKERS

[cr-ot-ch-wiss-kers]

The unfortunate creases that radiate from
your vadge after sitting too long
in linen or high-crease cotton trousers.

Dressology

COLOURKARMA

[cul-ah-car-ma]

Colour induced feeling of joy brought on by
wearing bright colours.

Dressology

CINDERELLA-WHAT-THE-HELLA

[sin-der-rell-ah-wot-ther-hel-ah]

An 11.55pm decision to actually buy that item
of clothing you have been eyeing on-line all day.
Next day delivery changes at midnight.

Dressology

CARDIG-ON-OFF

[car-dig-on-off]

That lightweight summer cardi that you put on
and take off all day as the temperature keeps
changing its mind.

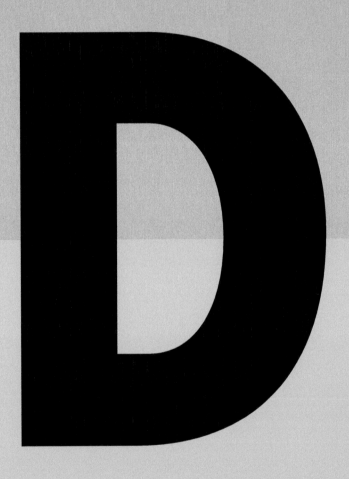

Dressology

DUNGARWEES

[dun-gah-wees]

When you inadvertently dangle your
dungaree straps down the loo and notice
a little too late.

Dressology

DE-STRESSDRESS

[dee-stres-dres]

Taking off that smart dress you've been
wearing all day and put on your comfy
home clothes.

Dressology

DOPPLE-HANGERS

[dop-pal-hang-ahs]

Clothes that you are automatically drawn to buy even though you have several very similar items hanging in your wardrobe already.

Dressology

ESPATHRILL

[ess-pah-thril]

The feeling you get as you walk out, summery
and sockless, wearing your new espadrilles for
the first time.

F

Dressology

FLUFF FLEAS

[flu-ff-fl-ees]

The multiple pieces of fluff that you find about your person and living on other items of clothing after wearing a woolly jumper.

Dressology

FAKEMENT PIECE

[fay-c-ment-pee-ss]

A stand-out item of clothing or jewellery
that is universally admired but cost you next
to nothing to buy.

Dressology

GRITE

[grr-ite]

The unattractive colour your white clothes or underwear goes when mistakenly washed with a dark item. Often used as a sarcastic expletive: eg. 'Oh grite!'

Dressology

GENUGRIN

[jen-u-grin]

The spontaneous smile you get when a
complete stranger compliments you on what
you're wearing.

H

HAIL-VARNISH

[hey-l-varr-nish]

When the colour of your nail varnish
announces your arrival before you do.

Dressology

HEMSTRUNG

[hem-str-ung]

When you can't decide what length
to make your trousers because you want to
wear them with both flats and heels.

H

HELLVET

[hel-vet]

When you make the mistake of ironing
anything velvet.

Dressology

I-COLOUR

[eye-cull-ah]

That one perfect colour, in any garment, that makes your skin sing, and your eyes shine.

Dressology

INVINCIBELT

[in-vin-ss-i-bell-t]

Finding that belt that suddenly gives you a
waist and makes you feel like a superhero.

Dressology

JUSTIBUYER

[juss-i-by-err]

The friend who always encourages you to
purchase something by providing
you with the perfect irreverent justification.

K

KNOCKERED

[noc-err-d]

When you try on a dress and your breasts
become the most prominent feature.
Sometimes good. Sometimes bad.

Dressology

LPD
(Last Pants in the Drawer)
[ell-pee-dee]

An uncomfortable affliction brought on by
having to wear the last pair of pants
in the drawer. Remember, they are always
the last for a reason.

M

Dressology

ME-THROUGH

[mee-thr-oo]

Items of clothing that reveal a little more of
your underneath than you first thought.

M

MISTAKEMAID

[miss-tay-k-may-d]

Inadvertently wearing the same coloured
dress to a wedding as the bridesmaids.

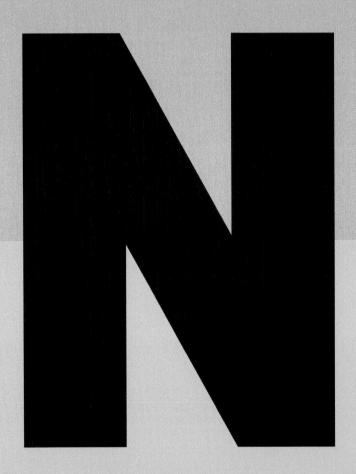

Dressology

NOTBLACKBLACK

[not-bl-ac-bl-ac]

When the black top you've bought to wear
with your black trousers is a different type of
black... not-black black.

Dressology

ORANGE-HANDED

[or-inj-han-ded]

The moment somebody catches sight of the colour of your palms after persistent fake tan maintenance.

P

PEDICLEAVAGE

[ped-ee-clee-vidg]

The tiny reveal of the start of your
big toe that frustratingly pokes out of your
summer shoes.

Dressology

POUND-PER-WEAR (PPW)

[pow-nd-per-wair]

The official way to successfully justify a very expensive pair of jeans.

Dressology

QUEUCULATE

[cuu-cer-lay-t]

Working out whether your potential sartorial
purchase is really worth the time spent standing
in the annoyingly long checkout queue.

Dressology

RETRO-GRET

[ret-row-gret]

The dull ache of lost love experienced when
you have decided not to buy that one-off
vintage find but can't stop thinking about it.

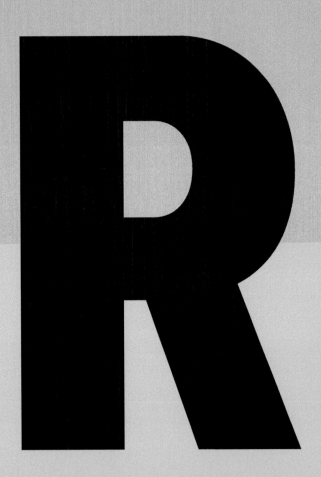

Dressology

RESHOEVERNATED

[re-shoo-ver-nayt]

When a fantastic pair of new shoes
completely updates the look and feel of
everything in your old wardrobe.

Dressology

SHATS

[shh-ats]

The crap hats that people wear at festivals.
Being under canvas does not give
you any excuse.

81

Dressology

SUBSLIDENCE

[sub-sly-denss]

The slow and irritating feeling of a bra strap
constantly sliding off your shoulder.

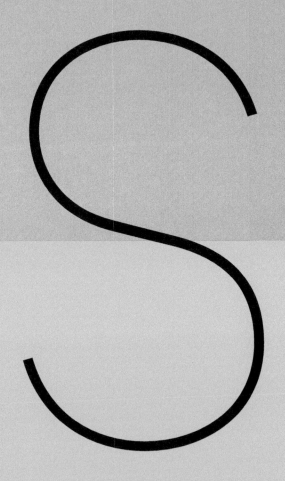

Dressology

SAUSAGESHINE

[sosh-idg-shy-n]

The unflattering shine given off by your legs when wearing tights with too much lycra in them.

Dressology

SWAYDY-LIKE

[sw-ay-dee-lie-k]

How you feel when you spend most of
your time in trousers and suddenly put on
a dress that swirls around you. Lovely.

Dressology

SHOE-STOPPERS

[shoo-st-opp-errs]

Shoes that demand a comment. Good
or bad, these shoes cannot be ignored.

Dressology

SECURITY BLACKET

[sec-yor-it-tee-bl-ac-et]

The faithful black outfit you always return to
for a dressy occasion. Colour would be nice
but black is always a banker.

Dressology

SLIP-SLOPS

[sl-ipp-sl-opps]

What sandals, slides or flip-flops turn into
after you are suddenly caught in the rain.

Dressology

SCANDALS

[scan-dalz]

Those uber expensive sandals that slice your feet to shreds the first, and only, time you ever wear them.

Dressology

SHUNNIES

[shh-un-nees]

Non-prescription sunglasses that cause
you to blank people inadvertently when
you're wearing them.

Dressology

TROUS-MOSIS

[tr-ow-z-mo-sis]

The technical term used when rainwater is
sucked up the hem of a wide-leg trouser in
wet weather conditions.

Dressology

TANFARE

[tan-fay-r]

The noise emitted by work colleagues as you come in, after a sunny holiday, wearing all white.

Dressology

TABRA

[tab-rarr]

The name, and joyful exclamation, given to the
magic strapless bra you've found that allows you
to wear off-the-shoulder-tops without the sag.

Dressology

UNAWEAR

[un-a-wair]

When your bag or coat has caught the hem of
your short dress whilst you are walking
along and you inadvertently reveal your pants
to the public.

Dressology

VERIFLY

[ve-ree-fly]

When the compliments you've received
on your new shoes/bag/coat/dress/top
confirm that it was a great purchase.

Dressology

WEBBED-THIGHS

[web-d-th-i-z]

An uncomfortable affliction that occurs
when wearing tights that are too small.

Dressology

WATERWEDGIE

[wor-ter-wed-gee]

When the sea does its thing to your new
swimwear. Not a good look.

Dressology

XSTYLE

[x-sty-l]

When you finally banish that dreadful
garment from your wardrobe that you've
never worn and only bought because
it was supposed to be 'on-trend'.

Dressology

YELLOHNO

[yell-oh-no]

When your beautiful egg yolk yellow
sweatshirt comes out of the wash looking
dirty mustard.

Dressology

ZIPOGA

[zip-oh-gar]

The core-strengthening stretch performed when zipping up a back-fastening dress on your own.

Thanks to Siobhan Mallet for inspiring this book.
And a huge thank you to Gary, Tom, Will, A.C. and M&D
for offering their wise council and super skills.

sim3allenkey.com

First published in 2019 by Great Curve

ISBN 978-1-912892-66-2
Design by Gary Cadogan
Printed and bound by TJ International
Project management by whitefox

GREAT
CURVE